The Voice of God Through the Eyes of *a Dove*

The Anointing From a Feather

Willowearth Convry

The Voice of God Through the Eyes of a Dove

Published by Revival Waves of Glory Books & Publishing
PO Box 596| Litchfield, Illinois 62056 USA
www.revivalwavesofgloryministries.com

Revival Waves of Glory Books & Publishing is committed to excellence in the publishing industry.

Paperback: 978-0692693797

PUBLISHED IN THE UNITED STATES OF AMERICA

Table of Contents

Chapter 1
A Child is Called by a Dove

Where this story begins and ends I have no clue your guess is as good as mine, I just know my doves will not stop cooing, so bear with me we will get through this somehow and right now I'm thinking how am I ever going to write a book.

My story begins in a field on my parent's ranch and me as a ten-year-old asking God for a job. I remember the day I asked, and the beautiful light that came over the field. I also remember the dove that spoke to me, but as a child, I didn't think much of it. I also did not know that thirty years later, that God would answer me, by sending me a dove that would change my life as well as others.

I was born to a Native American Indian Strong Elk. My dad had skin as red as an Arizona sunset. There wasn't much that man missed. He could read the winds and every rock. He had a way of reaching a broken horse and calm the storms within. It was not unusual for people to gather around my father and listen to him, he was a man who only spoke a few words, but at the same time, he put many words within a person's soul. I was born with the same gift that my dad was born with, at the time I didn't know he was from the bloodline that I will be talking about later in this book.

My mother, Lucia, was an old school Sicilian woman, eyes as black as coal. My mother was a whole five foot two, and she could hold her own. She had no problem dealing with a two thousand pound horse who is having a bad day; there was not much my mother feared. One thing about mom was when she was mad you better get out of her way, that five foot two women was just like a tornado that would swoop down on you, but boy where we loved, and boy could she cook

As children my father would take my brother and me into the woods and blindfold us, this was to teach us to know what part of the woods we were at, we had to rely on scent and our hearing. Let me give you an example, on how this works. The woodland has many different smells and sounds, my father would take us to a certain tree, so we could remember the smell, certain trees smells different because certain plants around it give off a different smell then, let's say other trees, so if we were in a certain place in the woods, we would know where we were just by the smell of the tree!. We would also know where we were because of the sound of a certain bird or animal who seemed to hang out in a certain area in the forest, and this is how we saw things without the help of eyes, and our first lesson on seeing within.

My brother was taking people out on horseback the one day, and when he was gone I picked up one of the chickens and held it in my arms, and when my brother got back, he told me he could smell that I was holding a chicken as well as knowing which one!

Growing up with a Native American father taught us to see with eyes closed, and how to read the books in all of God's creation. We grew up not only sensing the earth but so much more; we learned how to see without eyes. We learned about the stories that God put in the rocks. When Jesus went to the rock to pray before he was killed, he put his prayer into that rock, and in return, that rock shared his prayer with all the other rocks. We can hear the words of Jesus through any rock because his story was passed down by that holy rock. The wood that was used to crucify that beautiful man called JESUS also passed down his words to the other trees, so don't let anyone tell you can't hear the LORDS message on a tree or rock. Moses was spoken to by a burning Bush, and God once used a donkey to speak to Balaam, who refused to listen to God, so God spoke through his donkey.

You are probably wondering, what makes these doves so special. When my first dove flew into my life she spoke to my heart, that she was just one decent, of the dove that GOD

used to descend on his son, and there will be many more that are coming to the earth today, these doves are going out to the decedent's of the people from the lost tribe of Israel, some people claim that this tribe has, some Native American, blood in their family line there are many theories about this tribe. Some people also think that this is the tribe that came from Noah. Whoever they are, they are here today, and very soon will awaken through a call of a dove, who are decedents of the dove, that descended on JESUS, during his baptism

Chapter 2
The Coming of the Doves

Lucy felt her baby coming into the world. She yelled to my father, Strong Elk, stop talking to the tree, we are having a baby. As my father led my mother to the car, he looked up into the Sky's. He understood their language. A ray of light shined through a cloud, and a dove ascended from the clouds. My father knew it was a sacred day. He knew in his soul that it would be one of many doves to come. He watched it fly in a circle and disappear back into the cloud and back into the hand of God

As a child, I was very different, then the rest of the children. I grew up on a horse ranch, with lots of horses always around. Horses taught me a lot about the messages in the winds. They can feel the slightest shift of energy. If one horse feels something they all do, they were all very good teachers for me as well as my babysitters. I loved them and they loved me.

On are ranch There was a big pond on the property where us kids and snappers would swim. We never got hurt by them because dad taught us to emit a certain energy that would tell them we were not going to hurt them.

My dad once kept these killer Doberman's for a friend because his friend was going on a vacation and he needed a place to keep them. My dad said to tie them to a tree down in the yard and he would keep an eye on them. Well, little old I decided to go down and take a nap with them, and that is exactly where my dad found me, sleeping on the killer Doberman's and when he got close to me they growled at him! But they looked at me like one of their own.

The town I grew up in was a small town. A town where Mennonites grew their family and their crops and where men were still cowboys our town consisted of a mamma and poppa store a hardware store, which dad would take us to buy us kites. I always loved the smell of the hardwood store; I would always breathe the smell in, even to this day, and I can remember that smell. Our family Ranch is high on a mountain. Eight hundred above sea level. When it called for snow, we would get at least four extra inches and our road was the first to get iced up. Our town also had a tannery and a cookie bakery and my dad worked at both, so to say we are wired from the best cookies ever is an understatement.

Dad use to bale hay in the summer, and us kids would always help I can still feel the sharp hay between my toes and I would get hay splinters, I always ran around bare feet because I could connect with the voice of the earth more. In the Summer time talk about hard work, and I can still feel the corn husk scratching my skin and making me Itch? My Brother and I use to love to take the sweet corn from its husk and eat it raw," boy was that corn sweet."

Growing up around horses taught me a lot about myself, and instinct. You had to know when a two thousand pound horse was in a bad mood, believe me, you--- leave that boy alone, he wants nothing to do with you, and trust me you don't want to nothing to do with him either. Being in a field with many horses, you better know when to react very quickly. When a horse listens from within there is not much he misses, unless you're Stormy, who I will talk about later in the book. I have always been aware of the voice of the woods and how it spoke of God. There was a place I would go to as a child, It was hidden by very old, wise trees, you couldn't see it from the trail, but you could certainly feel it. My horse would hold his head up to the sky and take deep breaths; his body was always affected by the sacred circle and he could see what I couldn't he would start to prance and smell the wind. I would connect with his spirit to feel what he felt, and that's when I felt something very profound, I felt and knew by instinct that we came upon holy ground.

I swung off my horse, feeling the electricity of the earth meet my feet, as i walked up, I knew I had to make a pathway, so I jumped back on, okay boy, it's you and me, and we are going in, because that's how we roll.

In spite of many difficulties and my fearless horse spooking at imaginary monsters, we got to the clearing, after my horse bribing me to give him more oats.

In the distance, there lived twelve big rocks, in a circle, and each with its own story that God put into each rock. At the center stood a beautiful, strong oak tree. I could tell he had so much wisdom and would offer his wisdom, to whoever asked. I pulled some tobacco out of my medicine pouch and held it up to the four directions, then to the sky and the earth. Whenever a Native American comes upon sacred ground, we offer tobacco to send our prayers, and after I was done a beautiful golden eagle flew in a circle around the sacred place. I knew then it was a place that was calling me into it.

My dad always spoke of this place. He told me "when you are ready the place will call you." As I stood in the center, I felt electricity that sent a jolt into my soul. I closed my eyes and saw the beautiful stories within each rock, they all had a story to share with me, and they were all written by God.

If you are a writer and no one wants to publish your book, don't feel bad. These rocks never got their stories published, but one author did. His name is God, and he is the author of the stories within each rock, and the story within all of us.

On a Saturday night we would always find ourselves in New Holland, it was a horse auction where we would buy our horses for our hack string, we would take people out on the trails, and it wouldn't be unusual for my dad and brother to be out on the trail sun up to sun down. My dad would always say, whatever horse you dream about will eventually come through New Holland. And there were no truer words, believe me, he was right.

Chapter 3
The Beginning of Things Coming From the Sky's

As a child, I would always run like a dear, but with my eyes closed! I would Dodge the trees and rocks until one *day I smacked right into a tree.* I tasted the blood running from my forehead and lip, that's when I started to cry my mother, Lucy came running towards me, and took me into the kitchen and cleaned my wounds, only to find a little scratch, she asked me how I managed to smack into a tree I replied *all I did was open my eyes.* She looked at me and said I think me and your dad need to have a talk. That was the day I learned to close your eyes to see, because if you don't, you will surely smack into trees. "

The year was nineteen sixty-six, the year I turned two, and the year dad took me to my first Memorial Day parade. That was when I spotted the balloon that I just had to have ,after much persistence from me; dad got me the balloon. He had the clown holding the balloons, write my name on it, and I choose the white one with the doll in it. Out of the blue, a northern wind scooped up my balloon, and that is when my dad noticed something very strange instead of crying I smiled and said *bye bye I'll see you soon.*

Me and my mother were sitting on the squeaky wooden swing outside on the porch snapping green beans, when my mom noticed a balloon floating down the field, she watched it as it stopped right next to me, when I started to giggle, she felt her breath leave her body in shock when she saw my name on the balloon. My mother yelled for my father, who came out of the house with his cup of strong steaming coffee mom looked at strong elk and said *there is something very strange about this child.*

My father stood looking at the balloon; he knew other things would be coming from the Sky's and it wouldn't be balloons. The balloon came back to me a year later, and my dad knew it would be the beginning of things that would be coming from the winds and Sky's

As a little girl and having a gift and not understanding it, was very difficult for me. I could never pay attention to my teacher. I was always staring out the window and sensing a certain presence.

I use to sit under a very old tree that would speak to me about God, I would sit by this tree for hours, it was my best friend. Then there came the day when the teacher asked each child the name of their best friend. When she got to me, I told her my best friend is a tree. Everyone laughed at me, and the teacher told me I couldn't have a tree as a best friend. I left school in tears; I didn't understand why my best friend couldn't be a tree. And either could my dad. My father sat me down on his knee as I told him I'm not going to be friends with the tree anymore, because the kids laugh at me, and the teacher says I can't have a best friend who is just a tree. My father spoke softly to me and asked me who talks to you through that tree. I told him Jesus does, well isn't Jesus your best friend, I nodded with tears in my eyes. My father said, don't ever let anyone tell you that your best friend can't be Jesus. Later on in life, it was discovered that my school was built on a Native American burial ground, so I was the one paying attention, it was the teacher who wasn't.

When I started my first menses, is when my ability started to really develop and it started with the same children that use to laugh at me. Soon they were asking me about how I knew things, so the news spread about my abilities.

The kids use to go home and tell their parents what I would say. So the parents wrote a list for the children to give to me. With the increase of the gift, came the fatigue and the more readings I did, the more I was tired. It was not unusual for me to have many people around me in a circle, listening to the wisdom I shared with them, but doing this made me so drained that afterwards I sleep for hours, people would comment to my father how pale

I looked, and not to mention the most piercing headaches. There was one headache I never forgot, and it wasn't normal. My mom took me to the family doctor, who checked me out he saw my eyes were a little dilated. He took some blood from me and he noticed I had an increase of red blood cells, which I will share with you later.

Chapter 4
My Angel

I use to sit alone at recess; I still remember the cold, gritty, rough steps that I would sit on I loved to be alone because I could talk to one of the few friends who really understood me.

My friend's name was White Feather, and I met him and his horse, on the steps where I would sit alone at recess, the children didn't want me around them and that was fine with me. White feather had long dark hair, with very little silver in it. His eyes spoke of many truths and from his eyes came many words. I always remembered the eyes since I was to see them at another time in my life when a dove would stare back at me. He told me I must stand apart from the others for I was from an ancient race of people, which he called the *people of the dove*. Later in my life I found out *that there was a white feather in my father's family.*

White feathers horse was called Wind Walker and by far he was the most beautiful horse I have ever seen. He had every kind of feather woven up into his mane and tail. I absolutely fell in love with this beautiful horse, whose eyes spoke of many sacred things, and beside this horse always stood Jesus and White Feather.

Wind Walker was a brilliant shimmery white color and felt like satin, and that day on I knew that this beautiful horse would find me and call to my soul. White feather stood by his horse as the Lord walked over and told me when the time is right this horse would be passed down to you. *This horse has been passed down through many centuries, he is a very wise soul, and he is one of my beautiful creations. If I knew back then about stormy, I would have defiantly asked, what happened to stormy*

I asked Jesus, can I get the cowboy hat and boots to go with my horse. Jesus stood there smiling, then put his hand on my shoulder then vanished. Well, all I can say is I got my horse, but not my hat and boots, but I settled for just the horse.

Chapter 5
Mom Why Am I Different

My teenage years weren't that fun, I always had people around asking me questions, and the more they asked, the more drained I became, and there was no explanation for it. The increase of red blood cells increased with my gift. My doctor was confused about this and he told my *mom your girl should have so much energy because of the level of the red blood cells.*

It wasn't for many years later when I met a woman who could speak to angels, I had great respect for her and her faith in JESUS. One day I told this woman that after giving reading I would feel so weak and people would always mention how pale I looked after talking to people, and I told this woman who was called Leno, about it, she told *me thank God that you have the extra blood cells or you wouldn't be able to do what you do and live to talk about it, don't you understand the extra energy goes to support the gift, you need the extra blood cells to do what you do.*

My mother took me to the doctor the day I had another severe headache, that was the day I was doing many readings, and I almost passed out. Also, I started to see things differently from other people, like seeing halos, so the doctor suggested seeing an eye doctor to check my eyes. I remember walking into his office with all these machines around me; they could do everything but talk it seemed.

My doctor mentioned that my eyes were very intense dark eyes, he has ever seen, mom looked at him and said *she was born with my eyes and the first time I saw them I felt as if I was looking into my own eyes. The doc looked at her and said you mean after her eyes changed to the color they are now, she looked at him with a puzzled look and told him, no it was the day she was born and first opened her eyes.* He told my mom that's highly unusual and unlikely. A child's true eye color will show up later, the pituitary gland awakens and gives the child the right color, and the fact that your daughter was born with the eyes, she has now could mean only one other thing and that is that her pituitary gland was awakened already in the womb which some people call the third eye. He also mentioned that the halos that I would get are from an electrical impulse behind my eyes from a over active nerve end.

I would always come home crying from school, telling my dad everyone was calling me a freak. It would break his heart. He would always tell me to go to the woods since he knew nobody could explain, who I was better than the trees and the rocks that spoke the language of God and surely those rocks spoke, and I went to school telling the kids that I spoke to the winds and rocks, trees, and the creek that runs through our farm would sing to me. My mom told me you might want to keep that to yourself and stop listening to your father all the time, my dad looked at her *and said she better not keep it to herself. However God chooses to speak to her, is between her and God.*

I was ready to turn twenty-one years old in two hours, and I was sleeping, when my friend Bonnie and her husband came marching in, *wake up we are going out to celebrate. I picked up my pillow and threw it at them.* It didn't work, I went to the bathroom, slapped on some makeup, and did something with my hair, but to this day I don't remember what. I put on my cleanest dirty tee shirt that said *I love my horses, so you don't have a chance, and it* wouldn't be complete without my boots.

I came out of the bathroom, and my friend Bonnie said to me, you got to lose the shirt, I just smiled mischievously and said you're lucky I'm not wearing my chaps.

So there I was at a bar, and it just wasn't my scene, and out of nowhere I caught a glance of the doorman, as I felt lightning hit me, right then I knew he would be the one I would marry. And twenty-nine years later we are still together.

Chapter 6

GOD Releases a Dove From Heaven Named Mary)

It was a beautiful autumn day, where the leaves, let go of their trees so they can grow on the trees of heaven. That day there was a crisp feel in the air, and I could smell fall all around me, and the brewing of fresh Apple cider and pumpkin spiced coffee. Back in those days, the geese would migrate south for the winter, now they're too lazy to even migrate two miles if you're lucky, I'll tell you even the geese were different back then.

I walked out into the field and called my horse Wakee over; he came reluctantly because he knew he was going to be ridden. I took him by his halter and lead him into the barn with him sulking and arguing with me the whole time, I just looked at him *and said one way or another I'm getting on you so drop the attitude boy. Little did I know that I wasn't getting on his back.*

I grabbed a handful of his shiny white mane that was hard to grasp because the day before I put oil on it. I went to swing on, so I thought until he moved and I came down on my ankle talk about pain. I remember the barn boy and he was sweeping the barn floor, and I remember looking at the complete circle he made with the broom. I didn't know or really care at that time what it meant, but it would be a sign of something that would change my life.

I laid there crying until my brother came out and carried me into the kitchen my mom put some ice on it, I was thinking what a horrible way to spend my thirtieth birthday, this was certainly not in my plans, but it was in the plan for the man upstairs.

My sister Caroline who was as true as a cowgirl your ever going to find was out riding on the trail with her horse when she came upon a dove with a broken leg. It's in our family's nature to take care of anything injured. My sister got off her horse who was called Lena and gently took the dove into her hands and placed the hurt dove between her and the saddle horn, wondering why it was taking me so long, she decided then I wasn't on the trail and decided to head her horse towards the barn and help the dove.

I was hurting so bad from my fall, when I met Mary, I was so drawn to this little helpless dove, every day I couldn't wait to see her, and the only thing that kept my mind off my pain was Mary, a week later my mother took me to the doctor to get my ankle checked, the pain was getting a lot worse, and she noticed the skin looked different and that my ankle was cold. The pain was so bad I couldn't sleep, and the only comfort I had was my dove.

The doctor looked up at me from his glasses that fell part way down his nose. He told me the reason you have so much pain is from a condition called reflex Synthetic Dystrophy. He went on to explain that there is no known cure for the condition, and it causes the nerves to go haywire and send pain signals to the injured area that would make walking for me impossible *absolutely not what I wanted to hear.* So it seemed like my whole electrical system was different, and that also caused me to have heart palpitations, which is also caused by an electrical current. To come to think about it, my electrical system is very similar to a horse as well as a dove's electrical body.

My dove became my best friend and greatest teacher I ever had; I loved just watching her it kept me from focusing on the pain I felt. My father told me you might not realize this now, but that dove is here to let you know something that will change not only your life but the lives of others, and boy was he ever right I didn't know right away that she carried the words of God within her and that she was a descendent of the dove that God used to announce to the people that his son was the anointed one.

I would notice whenever I turned on the water spicket Mary would start to coo and her pupils would dilate, as well as her temperature and heart rate would also elevate. I also took note that before a storm would blow in from a certain direction, she would react differently to each wind and these are some of the things I observed

- ❖ North wind would make her pupils dilate
- ❖ East wind would make her feathers around her neck stand up.
- ❖ South wind would make her heart rate increase
- ❖ West wind would cause her to spread her wings as if to fly.

I also noticed that she would react to certain gems that I would wear it was as if she felt my energy being affected by certain gems and stones. I would sit with her at the medicine wheel. The medicine wheel is a sacred circle that the Native American people would go to pray, each rock would symbolize a certain direction, season, life stage, the four directions, and the plant and animals, and in the center, we would honor God by putting something special in the center. And God would call us to sit in a certain area so we could meditate on his words. The medicine wheel could answer any questions you might have, and give you guidance. It is a place where God speaks. At the end of the book, I will go into more detail about how to use the medicine and what the rocks represents.

As I was saying when I was walking around the medicine wheel asking God to point the way to the rock that I needed to hear, Mary would react to the stone that I needed to hear, her eyes would dilate, she would spread her wings as if she was getting ready to fly, and when I would study that rock and its meaning, it was right on the mark, that's when I realized that she is responding to my soul. By studying Mary I realized that doves respond to water as well as water in our bodies and since we are made up mostly of water, it can be affected by certain directions, and this is why doves have the ability to read us, in a way that's truly remarkable, because it is their own instinct, horses are the same way. I believe because having the same electrical makeup, I was able to figure out how doves and horses can be used for reading people. In the Bible, they call this discernment and that is one of the gifts that God gives us.

I decided to start using Mary to find answers for people. Later in the book, I will show you how it is done.

Soon it was time for Mary to leave, and soon it would be the time for me to walk again. Mary came to me in a dream the day after she died; she told me I would walk again, and every year on my birthday a dove would find its way to me. After the dream, I didn't have a lot of pain from my ankle so I tried to walk on it and I found the pain gone. And I could walk without the walker.

I walked right up our yard to where my parents lived they were so shocked, my mother almost choked on the orange juice she just made, she could not believe that after a year I was walking on my own we got into the car and drove to the doctor, who finally took off my ankle cast, and was very surprised when he saw a white dove feather inside the cast. He could not believe what he was seeing because people do not get cured of reflex synthetic dystrophy, but I did and my cure was God working through a dove .

Since then for twenty years a dove would come to me on my birthday and teach me how to hear God, and that beautiful man on that cross and how he got off of that cross. My doves that came to me where in the strangest ways, one year a person out of the blue brought me seven doves, it was the day of the saints, and it was when doves were given to honor the saints.

Another time on my birthday, I was demonstrating how I use my doves, to heal and read others, as usual, I had a line of people who came to see my doves and God working through them. And when I got some free time, a woman walked up with two beautiful white doves and asked me if I would take them, I told her of course I will but please sit down so I can give you a reading she kindly smiled and when I turned my head to look away and looked back at her to ask her something she was gone.

There were many more to come, but little did I know what they were going to bring with them. I had no idea at the time what these doves were about, and a holy race of people that would come to the earth near the end of days, and how these doves are to go out to the prophets of our day.

I was told this book will find these people, you are reading this because God put this book into your hands, you don't find the book it finds you, and so will the dove that God will release from his hand and give it one destination and that is to find you. And by the end of this book, you will find a feather that will lead you to the vision of a dove that came to me many years ago. The people of this race are very different listed below I will mention some traits

- ❖ Intense eyes, eyes that seem to see others for who they are, these people have a very faraway look in their eyes
- ❖ These people seem distant at times or unreachable
- ❖ They seem to speak with their eyes
- ❖ They have a deep connection with the earth and animals
- ❖ They might have a blood disorder or someone in their family, example anemic, rare blood type
- ❖ They seem to be attracted by birds and birds always are around them
- ❖ They are usually very spiritual
- ❖ They also have no problem reading people
- ❖ They are extremely affected by storm's
- ❖ They are born wise
- ❖ The children might get a lot of nosebleeds

❖ A lot of these people seem always to be tired as well as having a lower immune system

❖ Headaches

❖ Hormonal imbalance

❖ They seem to always find feather's

❖ They have a very strong electrical makeup

❖ Their eyes usually are more affected by bright lights

❖ These people seem to drain battery's very quickly

❖ Have the ability to heal

❖ Animals seem to find these people

❖ White animals seem to come to you in dreams or real life

❖ You are probably a decent of native American Indian, or the middle east

❖ You have had many doves come to you, or they build their nest near you.

❖ Usually, these people have an old tree that speaks to them, especially as children

- Your offspring, have a deepness about them
- You might have a birthmark of a circle or a cross or something that resembles a feather
- These people are drawn to the middle east
- They can get optical headaches, that causes you to see halos or bright colored zigzag patterns,
- Extremely affected by windy day's

Chapter 7
Calling of the Chosen

There was a slight chill coming from the breath of the north wind and a fresh scent that only a light rain can give off, one of those days that makes one crave hot chocolate. I'm no exception to the rule. Autumn time on the ranch is magical as well as beautiful. So I was looking forward to autumn and waited for the pumpkins and the silver coin to bless us. This is the time of year that I love making pumpkin bread and Apple dumplings (so if you need a good recipe, I can set you up).

I was walking into the barn with my usual bibs and my cracked leather boots, holding a mug of hot pumpkin spice coffee, taking in the spicy aroma and feeling the warmth of the scented steam hit my face. The horses looked at me like to say; *it's so nice of you to remember us and that we are in the barn starving to death.*

Yeah, right boys, boys. I just fed you guys an hour ago.

Well, if it's not too much to ask can we have some coffee with about fifty cubes of sugar?

Do you guys ever give up? Are you kidding me? Do you really want to get me killed or each other? Way too much sugar, guys. We will settle for one cube. But mom-

No buts, my decision is final.

Then through a distant wind coming from the north, I heard another voice that said, `` I will address you. ``I knew that voice. I had heard it throughout my entire life. The voice always ascended to me in a whisper of the north wind (the north wind is the creator wind).

"God, what do you want to address me about?"

I felt him breathe into my soul. You will write a book for me, and I shall breathe the words within your soul. I will release many doves from my hand that are waiting for certain people of an ancient race of people to hear my voice, for the doves are a descent of the dove I came in to let the people know that he surely is my son.

So I threw my horses out in their pasture, got some Apple dumplings that were still in the oven, took a plate out for me and I cannot do anything wrong horses, so they think, and I said, oh by the way we are going to write a book.

My Paso Fino gelding looked at me with his big, dark, can't- do- nothing -wrong look. We are going to do what? But mom, we can't even spell let alone write a book, and Stormy doesn't even know his own name or where he is half the time. But those apple dumplings look really good. Hope they're homemade with about fifty sugar cubes. Then we can talk

Chapter 8
I Don't Know Where I am Horse

I looked over at Stormy getting high sucking wood. Yes, you heard right. It is when's horse grasps wood between his teeth and sucks in air, and it causes them to release dopamine (known as the happy chemical) into their brain. They say it's a mystery why certain horses do it. Well, it isn't a mystery to me.

These horses like to get high, and that's exactly what cribbing does, besides being a rancher's worst nightmare, because they destroy fences. Believe me, when I say if Cheech and Chong had a horse it would be Stormy, yep, I can see him in the van with those dudes. I looked over at stormy as he was conversing with a rock. Stormy, what do you think of writing a book? He looked at me as if to say, *why do you think I'm having a conversation with a rock? We all know they have the books of God within them, for they are the story keepers of God.*

I had to smile. He was right. Then he headed towards the creek and stared at his reflection and started having a conversation with his reflection. I whispered to the illusion that this boy isn't right. The illusion replied, yeah, try living with him and his theories about life.

Where do I even begin to explain Cheech and Chong's horse, I mean this boy was definitely weird. My dad told me to go into his stall and have a talk with him; he told me you and him are both strange; maybe you can put your heads together and figure out the meaning of life together, or have meetings with the rocks together, very funny dad, we can try.

I walked into his stall. He was staring at the salt block like it was the most incredible thing he has ever seen, I thought to myself yep keep chewing that wood. He didn't even look at me. I thought, oh my God this horse isn't right. He is spacing out over a salt lick.

Finally, he took his eyes from the salt lick and stared at the water. Omg, *is this horse on acid?*

Finally, I said "Hey, you." Then slowly he looked my way. I thought, *well, I finally got his attention. Wrong. He was spacing out, looking at the hay, like he didn't know what it was.* I thought, *oh boy, what's wrong with you, boy?*

I decided to call him Stormy, because he had so many storms within him. Actually I should have called him I don't know where I am. Often I would find stormy staring at a tree, or rock and trying to figure out what it was. I'm not kidding. This horse was really weird. I would put feathers in his hair and flowers, and paint peace signs on him.

Chapter 9
The Dolls and the Amber Heart

My father died right after he bought Stormy for me and at the time, I didn't know then how important Stormy would be. In my horse therapy program, he helps a lot of people and teaches them about how to see the spiritual world. Stormy is actually highly intelligent, and even if it looks like he doesn't know what is going on, don't let him fool you. He knows more than you think. He is also a wonderful child therapist, for children who are different. He really understands and loves these children, and goes out of his way to help them, but most of all he loves God with all his heart.

The night my father died, he started chanting the Indian death chant. I remember that night. I was at a restaurant with my husband, and out of the blue, I felt drawn to go outside. I remember looking at the starlit night, and the beautiful full moon, that was so low in the sky, and it seemed like it was going to sit right beside me. I remember feeling sad, but I didn't know why. When I got home, I went to bed, and I had a dream that White Feather, came to my dad, he was leading the beautiful white horse, that was always with him. I remember my dad jumping on the back of the horse, looking at me, and saying, *child, look to the doves, they are coming*. After I woke up, the phone rang it was my mother, telling me my father died. The very same day my father died an Indian friend of the family that we have not seen for many years came up with Indian dolls. The weird thing was, as a little girl I wanted these beautiful Indian dolls, that all the children had, and what I got were Indian dolls made out of corn husk that my father would make for me. Boy, I now wish I would have saved them. So when our friend showed up, he didn't know my father had died. He said he didn't know why, but he found himself at an auction and for some reason he was drawn to buy three Indian dolls, two girl dolls and one boy doll, to give to us kids. They were the same dolls that I wanted as a little girl. *Thank you, daddy. I love the dolls, but I like the ones you made for me better.*

He came to me one other time. He rode upon the white horse I always saw with white feathers. I was crying under an old Willow tree when I saw him. He smiled and said, *keep your tears within you, I taught you better than that, then he went on to tell a story about an Indian girl, who stopped crying after her father died and for years she kept her tears dammed up. Then the day came when there was a very bad drought, all the plants and people and animals were dying. The chief came to the only one that could save the people and asked her the time has come when you must give your tears. The woman's eyes opened, like floodgates, and the tears flooded out of her and filled up all the creeks, and rivers, and through her tears, the people were saved.*

Then my father said, "this horse will be passed down to you, and he is coming soon." then he rode away into the four winds. I felt something hit my boot, and there lying on the ground in front of me, was an amber heart locket, and amber is made from trees, and my name Willowearth was also given to me by an old Willow tree that was struck by lightning four times and each time it was hit it grew even more. Let me tell you a little about the Willow tree.

Willow trees are always found around ponds or lakes, so they are very susceptible to getting hit by lightning, and when they do they die. But not the Willow tree that named me, instead of dying it got stronger with each strike. This tree taught me, no matter how many times you get stuck with something in life, you always have the power that God has given you, to not only rise again but become even stronger than before.

Chapter 10
A Willow Tree Who Gave Me a Name

I remember the day; my Willow tree gave me the name willowearth. I was sitting under the wisdom of this incredible tree, as it was teaching me how to use its branches to make a very powerful, spiritual tool. Which I will share with you later in the book. Sitting there, I heard willowearth, for that is the name you will grow into. One day I decided to look up the name, and I was shocked when I found out it meant wolferd in German. My father's last name used to be wolf bird, which meant Raven. Later on, the name was changed, 'which happened with a lot of my people ", , and it was changed to wolferd which means willowearth in another language.

Every now
and then,
something
comes into
your life that
is so good, so
pure, and so
raw, that you
know it came
directly from
God himself.

Chapter 11
The Angel and My Horse

One night I had the strangest dream. I was standing in the forest with the smell of lilac all around me, and a gentle loving wind that entered my spirit. There was a bright light in the distance, just like I saw when I asked Jesus for a job. I followed the light to an opening that led to a field, and I saw a round pen with a woman with a beautiful white horse. She wore, a shimmery white gown with gems and pearls, that's where woven into the sheer white gown. The horse, had a beautiful white sheer Vale over its body that seemed to shimmer a golden color in the sun. I walked up to the woman, and I asked her, how much is the horse. *In a very soft whisper voice, she said, child, nobody can buy this horse, it only comes from God.* Upon awakening, I forgot all about the dream, after I brushed my dark hair, I went up to the house to see the woman who called herself my mom.

When I opened the door, my mother had fresh Apple juice and eggs and bacon on the stove.

"Grab a plate kiddo we are going to New Holland, and grab some fresh coffee." Well, I wasn't going to refuse that. I learned a long time ago, never refuse food from an Italian woman, she will kill you lol

Before I even got my first bite of my crispy Bacon down, I felt my dad with me. I always had the ability to sense and talk with spirits. But this was very confusing to me. I worked with detectives on cases that involved talking to the deceased about who murdered them, and I have been always right on with solving the crimes. I just seemed to know things and I was very disturbed by it. I always let my doves work on cases with me, I couldn't have done it without them. I would always pray to the Lord to take the ability away, but the more I asked the stronger it became. And the one day, ''I told the Lord, *''Jesus, why do I have this, isn't it forbidden, isn't in the Bible that the dead are dead.*

Then I felt the presence of the Lord standing beside me

"Willow, Willow listens to my words, dear child." When I died on that cross, it was that you would not die. I vanished death on the cross; I did it so the ones who would be saved would come to me in the old testement it States that the dead are dead, but after my crucifixion, I rose. Then he told me he would give me truth. He told me to pick up the Bible and let him guide my hands. I excused myself from the table and took out the family Bible, and felt an invisible hand, guiding my hands, until I found the passage that Jesus wanted me to read. ''When Jesus died on that cross, the ground shook. The earth opened up and the Saints were risen, *(back then Christians today were called saints back then). The Saints went into the town, and were witnessed by thousands, and they ministered to the people of the town.* So the spirits that are with Jesus, have already risen, and the resurrection started the day Jesus died. And what we call psychic today, back in the biblical days it was called discernment.

A word of caution, ''be very careful contacting spirits, the devil, can disguise himself as an Angel, he is the greatest deceiver. Sometimes God will use a person to talk to spirits, that are in trouble, just like people who are alive, sometimes the devil tells these lost spirits to stay away from the light and not to go near it, he tries to keep a spirit under his control, that is why after Jesus died he went to hell, to free the spirits that were in prison. That's why I always use my doves for this kind of work and believe me, the devil doesn't stand a chance, with these doves around, they don't take any crap, excuse my language.

Chapter 12
Illusion is No Illusion

My mother's voice snapped me back to the here and now, and she said oh, by the way, we are going to go to new Holland today, because I know a horse is there waiting for you. Before I could protest, I found myself getting in the truck with the horse trailer attached to it. My mom started the engine. ''Uh, Mom, how about if I drive?

"Oh no, that's okay." Luey drives. "That's what I was afraid of. Luey was my mom's amazing wonder dog. Luey could do it all, according to mom. God, this dog is going to kill me yet. But I was hungry for the hot dogs that the auction was famous for, and even wonder dog, was not going to keep me from my hotdogs."

When we arrived in New Holland, I immediately took in the smell I missed so much. It was a combination of horse sweat, mixed with sawdust, and those incredible hot dogs with kraut. You, would always find the old cowboys talk about their rodeo days, and there cowgirl wives huddling together, rolling their eyes at their cowboys, and whispering to each other, here we go again, and the story always changes. Then I saw him, the most beautiful horse, standing outside the auction doors. He had a coal black, long shiny mane, and a beautiful silver tail. His eyes were so black and huge, and his pure white hair, set all the colors off. He was absolutely stunning. I knew this horse was already sold, but I felt myself moving towards him, and that's when our eyes locked, it is something I could never explain, but it was like we were one. I could feel absolute fear coming from this horse, this horse was beyond fear, he was broken, and my only desire was to un break him I asked the man, how much he sold the horse for. He told me he really took a loss, he sold him for seventeen hundred dollars, and told me the horse was worth, five thousand dollars, but he had to settle with what the man offered him. He really needed the money. I watched as a heavy set man, who was obviously drunk, walk over to the horse and slap him on the neck, and told the horse I'm going to get my money's worth with you. The man was also way too heavy for the horse. The horse's name was illusion De Mayo, he was a Paso Fino, and Paso's are little guys. This horse was so frightened looking at the man, that he started trembling, I could hear DE mayo say how will I even carry him, he will hurt my back. I looked over at Demayo who looked at me with tears in his eyes, pleading with me to not let him go, and believe me, I wasn't letting him go, illusion kept on moving closer to me and me to him. Then Jesus stood before the horse and gently petted the horse. Jesus looked at me and said have faith in me child, this horse belongs with you. Then out of the blue I asked the man if he would let me have the horse, if I offered him more money. He told me I don't usually do this, but the man gave me a check, and I just have a bad feeling about the guy, so if you can give me cash instead of a check the horse is yours. "I'll get the money. "I thought to *myself, did mom even bring five dollars for hot dogs? Maybe I can borrow from Luey.*

I walked over to my mother and she said, "did you see that beautiful white horse? He dances and everyone is saying they never saw a more beautiful horse come through New Holland. I didn't know he was a dancing horse; I just had this overwhelming feeling that God wanted me to have this horse. Mom, do you have two thousand dollars on you by any chance?

Well, you're in luck. I have brought exactly that amount of money, and extra for hot dogs, and thanks to Luey he told me to bring a lot of money, so Luey saved the day after all, **actually** he drives better than mom." **Now go and get your horse! I told you we were going to get your horse today.** *Mom, I will pay you back," yeah right, when do you ever pay me or Luey back.*

I walked up to where the man stood and slowly handed the money over. Horses are scared of any sudden movements, especially Illusion. The man took my money and asked if I wanted to ride my horse. Just those words made me want to pass out. "No, but you can ride him for me; I said. I asked about the man that originally bought illusion, "he told me he passed out in his truck. When the man got on him, illusion started to take off before the man was even on, but the man was an amazing rider. He showed me all his breath taking moves, as my jaw hit the ground, thinking, Dear God, I will never get on this horse.

The man brought illusion up to me and said; he needs a very experienced rider. He is very responsive and reacts quickly, and the only way to get to him is pray. Here young Lady. Here is your horse; and put the reins in my hand and walked away. I looked at illusion and he looked at me, both of us thinking, now what? Slowly I petted him. I noticed we were both trembling, but at the same time there was love, and there stood that beautiful man in the white robe, saying "Love each other, and do my work. "Now illusion works as a therapist, horse for abused women.

I led my horse to the trailer. I didn't even know how I got the courage to manage, but I got him home, he was very scared. I walked him to his new stall and gave him fresh water and hay and oats, he looked at me to say *thank "you"*. A couple of hours later I headed to the barn to see my beautiful new horse, with Luey following behind me. I looked at him and he was trembling and so was I, and thought, *oh brother, we are two of a kind. I wondered who was going to faint first _him or me.* Then, out of nowhere, I heard my daddy's words: ''Sit down in from of him. Look down and don't move. It will show respect. ''So, I found myself doing just that. Then Illusion did something that knows other horse ever did. He placed his hoof in my lap, and I felt the breath go right through my head. Well, at that point I thought I was a goner, but then I heard him say, "Take my hoof in your hand. "So I did. It was like we were holding hands, I felt like I was holding the hand of God through a horse. Then the day came when mom said, ''why don't you ride him? "I looked at her, turning white. ''Mom, are you crazy? You ride him or get Luey to ride him. I'll never be able to ride him. They tell you a scared person should never! Ride a scared horse, and I'm beyond being scared. Just thinking about it is making me have heart palpitations.

Mom looked at me and said, ″Do you remember the time we couldn't find you anywhere, and when we did you were fast asleep between killer dogs? And they loved you and you loved them, you were sleeping on them? They could have killed you. Instead, they protected you, like you were one of their own. Even when your father walked towards them, they growled at him. But you did something amazing; you had trust and faith that only a child knows. So get on that horse and ride him.

And I did just that, and he threw me off! I was sitting on him bareback because that was the only way I knew how to ride, and all the sudden he took off right from under me. I hit the dust, and that was the day I started to ride again without fear, He knew I had to fall to get back on and face my biggest fear, and I never stopped riding since.

Soon I was on his back, opening him up full throttle. Making fast turns and stops. People were so surprised, thinking, *thinking how does she even stay on that horse, bareback yet, nobody can even handle that horse except her? She was so terrified to ride for years, after her accident. Now she is the best rider we have ever seen.* They'd ask me, ''How do you stay on that horse? "I would smile and say because Jesus keeps me on. I learned that however fast life goes, and how many fast turns and stops. Believe in God and he will not let you hit the dust. Later on, illusion and I went on to showing and a two thousand dollar New Holland horse was beating out two hundred thousand dollar horses, and in the bleachers I always saw my dad and White feather smiling at me. People would comment, ''it's like you are one, it's not like we are one, ''we are one.

There was a beautiful sunset shining its light through the trees. It looked like an orange shimmer shining on the trees. Even the creeks shimmered with the glow. I walked out to the barn to get Illusion ready, for an evening trail ride, and I did something I usually never do unless I'm showing, I put a saddle on him.

After I had him all tacked up, I took him to the ring to warm him up before we hit the trail. When I put my foot in the stirrup, he was spooked, probably because he is not used to having a saddle on him and he wasn't used to it. So, he went to the left and my knee went to the right, and my foot got stuck in the stirrup. That's when I heard my knee pop. And that's why I hate using saddle's it's too easy to get caught up, and it also keeps you from connecting from your horse, actually once you ride bareback, there is no saddle that will keep you on better then bareback, you can feel your horse move better under you and feel when he is ready to spook. I went to try to get on him again, didn't think my knee was that bad, I went to get on and, "WOW! I fell to the ground, feeling my knee give out. Not good at all. I yelled for my brother to put my horse away, but I will never forget the look in Illusions eyes. He was so upset, because he thought it was his fault, that I got hurt, he is an overly sensitive horse. I petted him and reassured him that it wasn't his fault.

A couple of months later, with my knee still popped out (it still wasn't getting any better). I got on him bareback by gently lifting my leg with my hands so I could support my knee getting on. As I was riding him, he did something, he usually never does: he took off and started moving in different directions. Every time I felt I was going to fall off, he would move in a certain direction until I regained my balance. Then he stopped dead, and I went forward and almost fell over his head, and then I heard and felt my knee pop back in. It was like he knew what direction my knee needed to be pulled to pop back in. Here I thought I needed an operation, when all I needed was my sweet horse.

After I got Illusion, I bought another Paso Fino called Midnight. I was very drawn to him. This boy was coal black with a beautiful headset and amazing foot work. He was a very proud horse -to proud -and God help the man who he would leave on his back. He was the most headstrong hyper horse I have ever ridden. Everyone said that horse is going to kill you and I would just smile and then pray and hang on with all I had. Riding midnight, I realized that he reflected me and my free, unbreakable spirit, he reminded me of who I was, and to never give up being who I am, to trust in myself and always be a warrior, and you always give whatever you got to stand your ground.

Chapter 13
Wisdom Through a Dove

A rock medicine is a medicine from the earth and a gift of God. I learned about these medicines from the voice of God through the animals and the doves and horses. I have never read a spiritual book in my life, all of the things you will read about is from my own observations. *Do not use medicines to replace your doctor's instructions*

We will start with the four directions

1. North
2. East
3. South
4. West

The very first thing I do when I give a reading. I have a person connect with the eyes of my dove until I notice pupil dilation from the dove as well as the person. This is important because it tells me the light of

God is within the dove and the person. Below are the areas I use myself

Influential side detector

There is always one side of the body that is more influential, and once you know what side you are more in tuned with you can make a powerful impact with people.

The first thing I do is have a person cup their hands as I put the dove into their hands, then I will have them connect with the eyes of the dove *a lot of people feel a jolt of electricity go through them*

When a person has more water flow on one side of the body, that becomes their influential side, ''you are probably wondering well how you can tell that, ''I can't but doves can, and they are one hundred percent accurate. Let me explain a little about doves, before we move on. Doves have an ability to detect water movement, and electrical impulses, and when a dove senses moving water, it will spread its wings as if to fly, or open their beaks as if to drink water, and if your one side of your body a dove will be affected, by doing the things I mentioned above. When you hold the dove they will look at one side of your body, they will move their beak, and spread their wings, and their eyes will dilate all signs that the dove is responding to water movement. The reason they will be drawn to this is because if you have more water flow, that means you have a stronger magnetic field that causes the water and the blood to move faster. After I see what side the dove is reacting to, I write down the side for you, ''you might be thinking, well how can this knowledge help me, well a lot more than you think. So let's go into how the knowledge can help you.

Let's say you have an important meeting, and you want to really make a good impression.

Touch the person with the hand on the influential side, or have them stand on your influential side. Because your magnetic field is stronger on your influential side, it will also affect the others persons magnetic field.

Their eyes will dilate, their heartbeat and temperature will elevate. When this occurs it causes a person to be a lot more affected by what you're saying. Does this really work, you bet it does, its instinct from a dove. Now if you have a person always trying to stand on the opposite direction from the influential side, I can pretty much guarantee, that they are keeping something from you, people have instincts and they would intuitively know that the side that is less influential is less likely to pick up their deceit.

Now I'm going to go over how to make the spiritual and physical medicine.

As I mentioned above, there are four areas of the body you hold the dove towards, when a dove clamps her feathers close to her body, in a certain location of the body, that would mean, there is a weakness in that area of the body. That would mean the magnetic field is weaker, and this will cause the water to be slower. Slower water flow causes blood to not flow properly, and this will cause less oxygen, and that will cause miscommunication of the cells in that area of the body

These are what each area that is off can do

- **Head area-north _ headaches**
- **Senility or dementia, forgetting things**
- **Feeling like you are a burden**
- **Aging quickly**
- **Achy joints and muscles**
- **Lack of calcium**
- **Immature balding**
- **Increase of gray hair**
- **Feeling like you can't go on**
- **Fatigue**
- **Eye area -east**

- ❖ Your mind can't settle down, rapid thoughts that keep you up.
- ❖ Allergy's
- ❖ Sinus headaches
- ❖ Anxiety
- ❖ You are constantly thinking
- ❖ Optical headaches
- ❖ You have a hard time expressing yourself
- ❖ You are having a hard time communicating with someone
- ❖ You feel you are being misunderstood
- ❖ Thyroid problem
- ❖ Problems with eyes
- ❖ Making childish decisions
- ❖ Not thinking before you jump into something
- ❖ Impulsive
- ❖ Not asking enough questions
- ❖ Having problems with a child
- ❖ Not paying attention to the child within you

- Feeling overwhelmed

South heart chakra heart area

- Heart palpitations
- Skipping heart beat
- Feeling unloved
- Jealousy
- Circulation problems
- Having relationship problems
- Depression
- Anger
- Not believing in love
- Can't let go of someone
- High cholesterol
- Unexpected fevers
- Hot flashes

West feet area solar plexus

- Hormonal problems
- Moodiness'
- Bi-polar
- Diabetes
- Clinical depression
- Weird dreams

- Fatigue
- Feet and hip problems
- Water retention
- A need to be alone
- Delusional thinking
- Crones disease
- Irritable bowel syndrome
- Lower back pain
- Feelings of loneliness
- Sexual issues
- Feeling know passion with anything
- Boredom
- Laziness
- Escaping reality
- Very active imagination

How to correct directions that are off, in the body.

1. Let's say that the dove clamps her wings when she is held up to your

throat area (east). You would first go outside and face the *east *. You will walk towards the east, to you see a bird fly towards you that is very important!! Because that means something in the direction you need is increasing, your water flow and that means your water flow is increasing. A bird will always fly towards moving water. Pick up what is in front of you, it could be one of these things

2. **Feather**
3. **Rock**
4. **Plant**
5. **Twig**

Pick up what God puts in front of you, take it home and place it into a spray bottle, add some tap water, and spray on areas below

Beauty recipes

- ❖ Scalp it will increase blood flow to scalp _this will cause more blood flow to the scalp. More blood flow to the scalp increases hair growth, shine, and overall healthier hair
- ❖ Skin it will increase blood flow to the skin. More blood flow will stimulate collagen production. You will notice your face getting firmer, because the magnetic field increase and collagen increase, firms the skin, you will also have more of a glow to your skin. You can also use a rock in the direction that increases your blood flow. To do this take the rock and clean it off, place it into your favorite moisturizer for added benefits. You can also put it into your shampoo bottle. These two recipes are my beauty medicines I use, and it was all taught to me by a dove that came many years ago who took the time to

teach me this, I never read a book on any of this. I can tell you that you are going to be amazed with this natural beauty product. And it's all made by the instincts of a bird.

***Health Medicine ***

Spray your water on an area that is giving you problems. It will increase blood flow in the area and this will cause the area to heal. You can also spray your water into the bathtub and soak, this will increase blood flow around the whole body.

***Spiritual Medicine ***

Instructions

- **Go outside, and ask God, to bring in the proper winds**
- Face north-if you feel the wind blowing towards your face that would represent a **north wind**
- If you feel the wind on your back, it represents a **south wind**
- **If you feel on your right side, it represents the east**
- **Wind**

If you feel the wind on your left side, it represents the west wind

Where ever you feel the wind walk in that direction until you find a rock. Pick it up, and place it into a spray bottle. Add water

Areas to spray

- **Forehead awakens vision. It will give you clarity. And open up the third eye. It is also good for optical headaches**

❖ Spray around the ears. You won't hear a person's words. You will hear their unspoken words

❖ Throat area will awaken the sacred language, and give you the proper words. It will help you to communicate with people and animals

❖ Heart will heal broken relationships. It will also lead you to a soul mate, and bring back passion and happiness

❖ Stomach this medicine will open up your ancient DNA. It will also give you messages in dreams, and stronger instincts

❖ Feet. Add some olive oil to the water. Spray on the bottom of feet. This will lead you to find your dove, and put you on a path where you will meet your teachers and guides. It will lead you on a path that will lead you to find your answers.

- **Top of the head. This will open up the divine, and help you hear the voice of God. It will also help you to connect with loved ones in heaven and bring signs from the ones you walked this earth, before you, this is to connect with your ancestors.**

Wisdom soup recipes

These recipes are packed with nutrients, and very good for you. And they will cleanse the body. All you need to make these soups are your rocks, water, and the listed ingredients, you can put anything in your soup. You should also keep your rocks, to add minerals, to any type of broth, the flavor of the broth will get absorbed into the rocks so the rock will add flavor each time you use it. You can really feel the earth come within you making these soups.

- East wind soup. **Get a rock from the east, Put water in soup pan, place rock in water. For this soup, you want to add spring onions and tomatoes and whatever else you want. Bring to a boil. This soup is very good for sinus problems and mental fog. It will also give you clarity**

South wind soup

Choose a rock from the south. With this soup, add beans and whatever else you want in it. This soup is good for the heart and circulation. You might want to make this soup for a loved one to improve your relationship

West wind soup

Choose rock from the west. With this soup, add root food, like carrot, squash, pumpkin,

and whatever else you want to add. This soup is good for diabetes, and hormone imbalance. This soup is good for bringing messages in dreams

North wind soup

Choose a north rock. With this soup you would add Lima beans, and whatever else you want to add. This soup is good for clearing the mind, and for headaches. And bringing in wisdom.

If you need more information on the direction benefits, just look under the category for the direction meanings.

❖ Willow tree gift necklace

Willow trees are found around water. Their roots actually move towards a water source.

That is why you should never plant a Willow tree around a septic system. In the old days, people would use Willow branches to find water when water was nearby the branch the person was holding, would bend to where the water was located. This was called dowsing.

***How to make your necklace**

Get a Willow branch, bend in a circle, and tie your ends together and wear it around your neck

> ***What it does. The earth has water underneath the ground. The Willow branch will lead you to areas that stir the water in your body. This will make you feel you're in the right place at the right time. You will feel lucky.**

This necklace will also lead you to people that will make a difference in your life. 'and especially lead you to a soul mate. This is because the human body is made up mostly

of water. When you get closer to your soulmate, your aura will increase. Which in turn will increase water flow, the natural instinct of a Willow branch is to move towards whatever is increasing your water flow. A soulmate will affect the water in your body and the Willow branch will lead you to the area you are being affected by. One more thing if you wear this necklace around someone you love, it will increase their magnetic field this will cause pupil dilation, elevated heart rate and temperature of the person. When these psychological things take place, the person will be very stimulating, and intensely drawn to you. This is also good to where if you have an important meeting or job interview, and it works because it's that wonderful thing we call instinct.

Chapter 14
GOD'S Animals

❖ Did you know certain animals come to us at certain times in our life, or we become drawn to a certain animal? Then we look up the meaning and we are amazed at how accurate the animal message is. But do you know how and why it's so accurate? It is actually instinct. Let me explain how it all fits together.

❖ An aura color will change color when certain energy's come in. And believe it or not, different colors produce different scents. Certain animals are attracted to certain smells. So let's say doves are always around you that would mean your aura color at that time will have a lot of white. Certain animals are also affected by certain colors.

❖ Animal meanings

Bear /

Knowledge and wisdom are coming your way, follow your hunches and instinct

Rest and meditation are needed at this time

Keep a low profile

A crystal will come to you soon that will awaken your bloodline

Dreams are very important at this time

Medicine men and women are under bears influence

Deer/

Pay attention

Think before you make a decision

Be gentle with yourself and others

Love will find you soon

Be alert

Pay attention to your senses

Horse/

Break away from what's in traps you

Don't let anyone break you down, or try to control you

Don't brush away feelings you have

Someone will support you

You will be led on an important path

People right now are very drawn to you

A powerful connection is coming your way

Native American past life

Trust in your feelings

Dove /

Divine knowledge is coming to you

Angelic experiences

Ancient bloodline from Jerusalem

There will be a miracle from God

You should go into healing work

Mentor and guides are coming soon

You will meet someone who is your Angel

There will be peace and powerful love coming

Look into the Bible at this time; a very important message is coming from Jesus

A passed over loved one is sending healing feathers to you, and giving you signs

Hawk /

A circle symbol will be an important sign

A message is coming soon

You will receive clarity on a certain issue that you might be dealing with

You will receive good news

You will get a message by phone, text or email. That brings a new change in your life

A man spirit is connecting with you

It's time to complete something

There will be a new birth

Cat /

Patience is necessary right now

Study up on something

Egyptian bloodline

Keep a close eye on things around you, and people

There were women in your family; that's where known as wisdom keepers

If you are suspicious of something, your instincts are probably right

You have a very mysterious way about you

Your eyes carry ancient wisdom and have a deepness and intensity about them

Someone is very confused where they stand with you

Owl/

A very important book will come your way that explains who you are

Now is the time to be silent and observe things around you

You come from a very powerful line of women

Look deeper into things

Someone is ready to go home

You will what is going on with someone

You will be giving clarity into the storms of life

Wolf /

You are on the right path

You will feel the earth messages

Be loyal to what you believe in

Through persistent you will get what you need

You need to walk alone at this time

Trust your instincts

You will find your path

You will lead others or become a leader

Observe things carefully

Eagle /

Victory is coming to you

You will succeed

Listen to the words of a child

Your perception will because very strong

You will see and feel thing coming from a distance

You will receive much clarity with people

People will be inspired by you

You will achieve something that makes you happy

You might want to learn a new skill

Ravine or crow /

Warn others if you feel they're making a mistake

You will be given something that you need, just like Elijah was fed by GOD through ravines

Ant/

You will find out you have more strength than you think

More responsibility is coming your way

It's important to work with others

Now is the time to start projects with others

Family structure is important right now

Working on family projects is a good idea now

Turtle /

Slow down!

Start on house projects

Gardening will be very relaxing for you right now, or goings-on nature walks

Don't rush new projects

Native American DNA

The Native American spirit guide is leading you

Bison/

Sacred teaching is coming your way

It's time to make certain sacrifices

Believe in your prayers

A prayer will be answered

Geese/

Your timing will be perfect

You will soon be very in tune with someone

A place you go to can give you a healing

There is an important person who lives around water

A vacation will be a blessing, and going on this vacation brings wisdom

Dolphins or Whales/

Someone will keep your head above the waters

You have an ancient connection to Atlantis

You will find a seashell that will awaken your memory of Atlantis

You will get out of deep water's

Listen to your emotions

A person who is ill will get better

You will start to see your hard work pay off

Butterfly /

Transformation

New change

New love coming to you

Someone who is an artist will enter your life

Your creativity will increase

You will get a project off the ground

Plant your ideas

You will be lead in unexpected ways

Spider /

Watch out for a trap

Don't let someone control you

Someone is being deceiving

So will receive something written that will be important

Don't get caught up in someone's Web

Learn something creative that you always wanted to learn

Beaver/

Being alone right now is needed

You need to work alone on a project

Be persistent with what you want to find out

You need to dig a little deeper to find your answers

Being around water will bring you vision and reflection

Hummingbird

You will be able to do something you never thought possible

You would be very good at working with flower oil's

You need to have faith, don't give up because someone says you can't do it

Snake/

Someone very colorful and charming are not what they seem to be

Someone is not telling you the truth

Someone around you has very bad energy

Someone can strike out at you unexpectedly

Don't trust what you hear

It's time for you to shed your old ways

Someone from your past will return

Fox/

Someone is being sneaky

Protect your belongings

Someone could be trying to manipulate someone you're close to

Someone could be watching you or a loved one

Coyote /

Trickery

Don't complicate things,

Don't trust a person who says they're going to change

Stop making excuses for someone

Blue Jays /

Happiness is coming to you

You will make good choices

Robins /

New beginning

New growth

You will be giving an important sign

A child is going to be born around you

You will have a stronger connection with a child

You and a young person will become closer

Marine life/

Your psychic abilities will increase

You will become part of a group that supports you

You will be lead to a seagull feather, keep it with you it will help you to find the answers within

Where a seashell necklace at this time it will bring new creations to you

You will feel your bloodline awakening in you

Frogs /

It's time to cleanse yourself from people who are dragging you down

Rid yourself from situations that are not good for you to be in

Chapter 15
A Feather Released From the Hand of GOD)

- **The vision feather**
-

Right after you finish this book GOD will release a feather from his hands and into yours. Upon receiving your feather. Put it into a spray bottle, add some olive oil. Once you do that, you must get a cross. Place all items in a spray bottle and add your water, if you can get Holy Water, from a minister that would be ideal, you should also put rose petals in the water.

Spray the bottom of your feet, and this will lead you to the dove that God has chosen for you. Also, you can use this sacred oil on your feet to lead you to people and things that are part of your calling. And also lead you to sacred things

❖ How to find your dove, and how to prepare it

The first thing you should do is pray to Jesus to lead you to your sacred dove. What I recommend is for you to check out bird auctions in your area, or you can do a check for dove sales.

How will I know the right dove when I see it?

There are several indications and behavior that your dove will display

- ❖ Spreading its wings
- ❖ Staring into your eyes
- ❖ Fluffing of the feathers
- ❖ Walking in a complete circle
- ❖ Ask the salesmen if you can hold them. Usually, they will let you hold them the one who feels warmer than the rest is a very good indication, or if you feel a stronger vibration from a certain dove.

Cooing or if they look like they're bowing to you

How to prepare your dove for its special job

It's very important to have a reasonable size cage for your dove, make sure you ask what kind of seed they use to feed their doves*they love saffron seeds*.

Make sure they have fresh, clean water. It would be really important if you can keep their cage beside your bed at night, this will allow them to give you gifts and blessings as you sleep.

I also can't stress enough that you hold them to your heart that will comfort them and you. You should also look into their eyes because that will bring in the eyes of GOD. Take time to talk to your dove, and ask it for its name; the name will come to you. Put a BIBLE by your dove, and hang a cross on the cage. One last thing you should do is put a crystal of your choice, in their food dish or water dish. You are now ready to help others find their way back to God.* God bless you and your dove *

How to do a medicine wheel using your dove

Place four rocks in a circle and one, and the dove in the center for GOD.

Spray each rock with the water you made to find your dove

- **You need to find four rocks**
- **A rock in the north direction**
- **A rock in the east direction**
- **A rock in the south direction**
- **A rock in the west direction**

- **Place your north rock in the north**
- **place your east rock in the east**
- **place your south rock in the south**
- **place your west rock in west**

Place your dove in its cage in the center to represent the GOD.

Ask yourself a question, walk over to each rock, when you see some type of reaction from the dove, sit down at the rock and look into the eyes of your dove then trust in the answer that comes to you, then read direction meanings below and the animal meaning, listed in the book And use the rock associated with the directions, to bring in more clarity of the direction (place a rock in a bottle of water, and drink the water)

DIRECTIONAL ROCK MEANING

North alabaster rock

Winter time

Elder

White race

Bison and snow geese

Earth element

East Citrine rock

Springtime

Child

Yellow race

Hawk, eagle, butterfly, deer

Air element

South rose quartz

Summertime

Red race

Adolescent

Wolf and horse

Fire element

West onyx

Autumn

Black race

Adult

Bear, owl, raven

Water element

Directional Attributes

North

Knowledge

Wisdom

Letting go of old things

Renewal

Sacrifices

Teachings

Mentors

Completion

East

New beginning

New birth

Creativity

Ideas

Communication

Vision and clarity

You will have a reason to celebrate

South

Love

Friendships

Rapid growth

Trusting in yourself

Healing of the heart

Travel

Commitment

New found passions

West

Rewards

Reflections

Your hard work will pay off

Finding out important things

Past life connection

Past life

Pay attention to dreams

*If you would like more information on the medicine wheel. I highly recommend

Dancing With The Wheel from Sunbear*

Chapter 16

Some Times Angels Come on Windy Days

These are some very beautiful story's I love to share with you.

Windy was a beautiful white Mustang with big dark, soulful eyes and no one could ever break his spirit, and what kind of person would ever want to do that.

Windy was a very unapproachable horse, but a gentle soul. Even though he was beaten by a man, he still loved. Windy was like the wind and it took me a year just to pet him and let him know he was safe on my ranch with me. I loved him and he loved me. I was giving a healing reading to a woman using my horses, and I kept on glancing at the little girl who was very sick. When I looked back to where she was sitting, I couldn't find her. Nobody knew where she was. I panicked when I saw her pelting windy, but the wind did not move away from her instead he followed her, and kept nudging her, after about fifteen minutes, the little girl said goodbye to windy, but that was not going to be their last visit with each other.

A week later the little girl told her mother that the white unicorn would come to her in her dreams and take her to a magical forest where Jesus would ride with her.

Two weeks later they took her to the doctor to check her blood cell count, and when her results came back, her leukemia was gone.

There is another story I like to share with you about a Hindu woman.

It started when she went to visit her family in India and when she came back to the states is when her left arm became paralyzed, within one week she lost complete control of her body. She became completely paralyzed from the neck on down.

Her brother owned a Convenient Store not far from where I live. He remembered a woman in a white dress come into the store and noticed that she seemed very Angelic, she looked at him and handed him my business card, without saying a word, and she left. He took my card home and called me. I answered the call as I explained that I use doves to heal people and give readings He explained all about his sister, and told me they had seen the best doctors in the states and in India, no one knew what was causing it. I told him I would bring my doves, to her.

The first thing I saw was this beautiful young woman lying on the rug unable to move; I remember she gave me a smile that seemed to light up the room. I immediately went to her and held her hand. I told her family that it is a bacteria from chicken, then I asked them if she had chicken before they left India, the answer was yes. I gave them a name that came to me and asked them to check with the doctors in India if they ever heard the name I wrote down. There was one old doctor who recognized the name, He mentioned it is from a bacteria in chicken that causes paralysis, but there is now known cure, and eventually it will affect her heart and breathing. Usually, the person doesn't live long. They called me back over again to use the doves on her again because after the first time she was able to move her arm. I brought my doves over and let them sit on her as her family watched in amazement, as the doves spread their wings over her body. I put the doves back in their cage and held my hand out for her to hold on until she took my hand and I asked her to stand and with a little help from her family, she finally stood up. Today she is walking and the paralysis is completely gone as I'm even writing this my doves are cooing. I can't explain what happened that day, but I'm putting money on the doves.

Chapter 17
Questions and Answers

Question why are these doves different

Answer GOD told me that these doves that he will release from his hand are decedent's from the dove that GOD sent, to come to his son to mark that Jesus was the anointed one, and the son of GOD.

Question
When will I receive the feather?

Answer
It should come when you finish the book

Question
How will I be able to know my dove is the chosen one for me?

Fluffing the feathers that makes the dove look like he's puffed up, this behavior is very similar to getting goosebumps.

Spreading of its wings

Walking in a complete circle

If you can hold the doves look for the one who feels warmer than the rest, or seems to have more of a vibration, it will actually feel like the dove is vibrating or trembling

Pupil dilation

Staring into your eyes

Feeling cone teddy to a particular dove

And the dove should be white

Question

Do you make medicine boxes up for making a medicine wheel to use?

Answer

Yes, you would contact me so I can have a free consultation with me to see what is needed for your type of energy

Question

Do you do personal readings, using your doves and horses?

Answer

Absolutely

Question

Is there really a reason for being drawn to this book?

Answer

You bet there is. You have a holy, sacred bloodline that goes back to Jerusalem; some people call this the lost tribe of Israel.

Question

What am I supposed to do when I get my dove?

Answer

The dove that comes to you will instruct you. Before you go to bed look deeply into the doves eye's, upon awakening, you will know that answer

Question

Can my dove do miracles?

Answer

You better believe it you will be amazed at the ability of these doves.

Question

Does God work through these doves?

Answer

He sure does. Looking into the eyes of your dove will feel like you're looking into the eyes of GOD, you will also hear the voice of GOD through the eyes of your dove.

Question

Why has GOD sent these doves to the earth?

Answer

From what the Lord told me, he sent them to gather his prophet's and the saints of our day.

Question

How do I get in touch with you?

Answer

My email

willowearth29@gmail.com

website voiceofgod.simdif.com

My website

Http://voiceofgod.simdif.com

Phone number

484-575-7138

484-772-9240

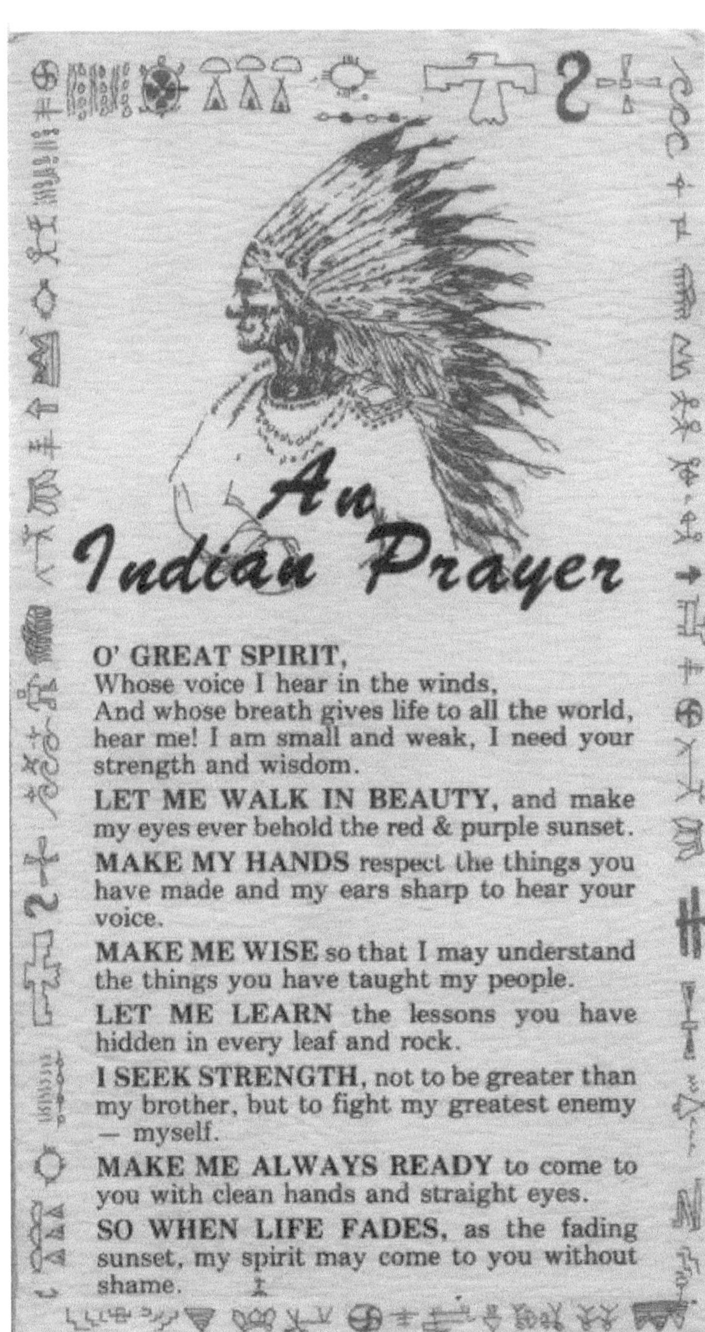

An Indian Prayer

O' GREAT SPIRIT,
Whose voice I hear in the winds,
And whose breath gives life to all the world, hear me! I am small and weak, I need your strength and wisdom.

LET ME WALK IN BEAUTY, and make my eyes ever behold the red & purple sunset.

MAKE MY HANDS respect the things you have made and my ears sharp to hear your voice.

MAKE ME WISE so that I may understand the things you have taught my people.

LET ME LEARN the lessons you have hidden in every leaf and rock.

I SEEK STRENGTH, not to be greater than my brother, but to fight my greatest enemy — myself.

MAKE ME ALWAYS READY to come to you with clean hands and straight eyes.

SO WHEN LIFE FADES, as the fading sunset, my spirit may come to you without shame.

SD - #0020 - 070726 - C0 - 216/138/7 - PB - 9780692693797 - Gloss Lamination